I See Your Point

Understanding Others

Leigh McClure

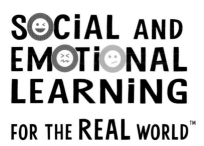

SOCIAL AND EMOTIONAL LEARNING FOR THE REAL WORLD™

Rosen Classroom™

Have you ever disagreed
with someone?
Have you ever felt differently
from someone?

Maybe you believe in one thing.
Your friend believes
in another thing.

How can you fix the problem?
Listen to one another!

Your friend believes soccer is best.
You believe basketball is best.

Listen to your friend.
Try to see their point.
You don't have to agree.
Just understand!

Maybe you feel one thing.
Your friend feels another.

You feel happy at a sleepover.
Your friend feels scared.

Listen to your friend.
Why are they scared?
How can you help?

You can say, "I see your point."
Let them know you understand.
Be there for them.

Try to understand others.
All you have to do is listen!

Words to Know

basketball

sleepover

soccer